A Safe Place

A Safe Place

Poetry Collection
Written by Rory L. James

Any connections are entirely coincidental.

First paperback edition June 2023

Book design by Rory L. James via Canva

ISBN 9798391135395

*Dedicated to those that deconstructed me so
entirely that I had to reconstruct my
understanding of reality.
But more importantly, the few that kept me
alive in the process.*

Contents

I. Naivety

Contents

II. Chaos

Contents————————————————

III. Broken

Contents

IV. Resilience

Success

Success
does not look
  how I expected.

It is not
  always visible—
sometimes
  success
can be
  staying alive.

NAIVETY

Naivety

Trusting the construct of love
Longing to love and be loved
Neglectful attachments in the past
Relationships that didn't last

Each of these reasons can exist
before an abusive relationship
and can cause someone to not resist
accepting toxic love.

Home

Seeking a home
in a person
instead of a place.

When people
are as barren
as abandoned shacks.

And my own body
longs to be lit
with a candle
and made
into a home.

Chasing Wind

The wind
feels like home
and so
I'll let it blow me away.

Blue Little Bird

Blue little bird
trying to fly
Mom never showed her
but she's gonna try.

Blue little bird
reaches the sky
and she glides—
soaring so high.

Blue little bird
she lets out a sigh
ecstatically clinging
to whoever else flew that high.

Blue little bird
is set up to cry—
Mom never showed her
how to find a nice guy.

Conflicting Passion

You say I am the one for you.
You show that I could never be.
But you kiss me like it's true.
The hot sun burns my skin,
makes me feel alive;
hurtful love,
like you.
I'm alive, loving the sun
that burns me
so maybe—
I can love you too.

Condition

I love you
    unconditionally.
You love that
    conditionally.
But love heals
    infinitely.

I can fix you.

Listen

When someone warns you
of their character, listen.
Do not infer their insight
as adequate evidence
that they are not innately evil.

Yes, good people do bad things.
But, bad people do good things.

They know they are bad
and by warning you
they are excusing themselves
of the reckless heartache
that they know will inevitably
ensue upon you.

Yes, you *could* change them.
But, they will probably change you first.

Moonlight

The sky has always fascinated me
the stars rest in the void of night
the same way the sun rests in
the vivid bright. Relationships
steadily intertwined; different
yet connected at the same time.
If I were the moon I could
light up your dark. Would you
settle and rest, as I dimly shine
on your empty parks? Or would
you half, quarter, and crescent
my glow,
> —*would you phase me*
> *until my light goes?*

Moth

A moth flutters
by an open flame
      burnt to ash
      before it could feel pain.

Dangerous naivety
      strikes again.

Merciful flames
that burnt my skin
a warning for me,
      a moth perished in.

History Repeats Itself

Poetic essences of embellished truths
become beautiful lessons read by the blind.
Experience is a prerequisite in sooth
because resonation within youth
requires a compilation of time.
History repeats itself sevenfold
through all of the stories that are told;
The Great Depression, The Great Recession,
sinking ships from blocks of ice,
school shootings, Bonnie and Clyde.
Tragic even, though they be,
experience is a fickle thing.
And most imperatively it seems to me
the tragedy of your words to me.
"I'm sorry," after broken glass,
"I will change, it's in the past."
Apologize and break my phone,
leave in fear that you broke my hipbone.
Oh, the tragedy of so many lives lost,
the selfish reframe of my youthful mind
proclaiming your abusive charms as a crime.
The grief that freezes through my heart
is the cycle of abuse that I never saw start—
history repeats itself every day.
I cry for my daughter's role to play.

Wild Child

You've always been a wild child
                under the sun.
You've always been inclusive
                to everyone.
You can be wild
                the world will stay.
You can be a child
                just play.

Unhealed

A lost little boy can't even tend sheep
he's trying to survive just like a man;
busy looking for food, a place to sleep;
this limits him to walk, while others ran.
Limited potential from his mistakes,
he'll never tend sheep or find his own meal
success detrimental, life or death stakes;
trying to survive, *not trying to heal.*
History of trauma litters his past
all while thinking that he has outgrown that;
clouded judgment and perspective outlast
stuck in his personal mental combat.
He'll disappoint everyone love involves—
unless his internal conflict resolves.

Fire Footsteps

Burnt-out fire footsteps in overgrown grass
someone already journeyed this path.
I know it. Still, it feels lonely.
Like it's my origin, my direction only.
I remain walking. Choking on
the fragrant air of a candy sky,
sugar-coated twilight. Rots my teeth,
puts stars on my skin. The itchy heat
consumes me and causes me
to repeat my family's history.
But the breeze tastes sweet. I remain
walking, each step burns. I wish
that I could just go home, please.
This trail delivers me from my adult life and
towards my past. Lost, but self-aware,
I remain walking. My disappointing
childhood led to my aspirational life terms,
and yet I inevitably repeat deleterious
generational patterns. I remain walking.
These footprints, I have known my whole
life, I pledged that they would never be
mine. But no matter how far I walk— I
circle back, please make it stop.
I remain walking, my daughter's hand in
mine, while my footprints reduce to ash.

Storm

I will make
your voice thunder
and spark your soul.
Lightening
that can start a fire
consume miles.
I will make you feel alive.
Ashes, charred rubble.
Voices yelling, thunder.
I will make
your eyes rain tears
that quench oceans.
I am a storm
I will never be quiet;
thunder and lightning,
fire and rain.
I will make
you feel like one too.
I will make
you feel all of my pain
— toxic passion.

Paradox

I love conflicting company;
peaceful loneliness,
confident insecurity,
calming anxiety,
romantic torment
          —comfortably hurt.

Shapeshifter

Forcing myself
into a box
minimalist
contortionist
shapeshifter
what am I now?

A Challenge

You were supposed to be a distraction,
I didn't expect the attraction,
I will fight it.
You intertwine your fingers with my fist
I forget how to hit
deflective protection I can't resist.
Trusting your touch
as a protector of all
but I'm holding your hand,
what others would call
a weapon.
And it feels like
I have tamed a beast
because I know
you'd never hurt me.

Graveyards and Ghosts

I am not scared of graveyards and ghosts;
I am scared of being alive while alone.
I am scared of love, that it will not last,
of being rejected, of sharing my past.
So when you like me and ask about my day
I just want you, please, to go away.
And yet, I also hope someone would stay.
You tried, it scared me,
I don't know what to say.
And so I ghost you,
and I'll ghost the next one,
your number saved next to the last one.
A few ghosts together, a graveyard it seems,
and so it appears I am scared of these things.

I am scared of graveyards and ghosts.

Youthful Romance

I watched your eyes light up
in the summer rain
seduced by mischievous nature
under the stars, you whispered pain
fears were always your wager.
I accepted the challenge, sevenfold
lost in the comfortable chill of summer
I longed for you to permanently hold
youthful romance couldn't be any dumber.

Savage Gaslighting

I was too young to understand
that wolves dress like sheep
to prey on the weak.
But they wear the wool for so long
that it covers their eyes
they forget that they're wrong
and what lurks inside.
They still have sharp teeth
they'll still make you bleed;
but they'll act surprised
when they make you cry.

Loyalty

You can show love in many ways,
but I think my favorite is choosing to stay.
I won't give up on loving you.

Loneliness

She wears her truth as skin and wraps
herself in the warmth of your lies—
she knows, she just doesn't want to be cold.

Love

Love can be real
it's in the melody of the leaves
rattling together in a cool breeze
it's in the solace of the night
and the welcomed starlight.
If love wasn't real
the birds wouldn't sing
and my heart wouldn't feel
like it could heal anything.

CHAOS

Chaos

My relationship changed,
I don't know when,
I just want it to change back again.

Once boundaries have been crossed, things become confusing. There are a lot of conflicting feelings and a lot of denials that prevent processing all of those emotions. There are a lot of *what-ifs*, that can cause hopeless hope and self-blame, mixed with embarrassment and a need to conceal.

There is also love and kindness in the thick of experiencing abusive behavior. This redemptive behavior feels like a dopamine release, a significant reward that lingers. Until the next arbitrarily hurtful thing steals that sensation in seconds. Momentary love and momentary loss are so intimately charged.

He's the only one I would stay for.
I left and came back, this time will be
different.

Monster

You told me you were a monster
I told you, "You could never be."
You were scared of hurting me
but not scared enough not to.

You were not always the monster,
you feared it.

But you allowed it to consume you,
and so
        you
                became
                                it.

Self Doubt

Invasive thoughts
      when it's quiet
time to think
      and I allow it

When you yell,
      rip out my soul
when you're rough,
      cauterize the hole.

You say words,
      not take them back
and then talk sweet
      ignore the bad.

Tired of assaults
      in private
but I feel *relief*
      when I allow it.

I apologize
      for all that's been done,
I'm sorry, but,
      I'm the only one.

Anything

I could
do anything.
Push my needs aside?
I would
do anything.

Just don't,
let me go.

Demons

You're charming and charismatic
with demons hiding in the attic
dark nights, dark home;
you're a lost cause, you have no soul.

Every day you make me laugh,
and every night I want that back.

I know you're gone
this is a trap
but I'll play along
I'll have you back.

The charming and the charismatic
until your memories make you manic
dark nights, dark home;
I'm a lost cause, you broke my soul.

Critical

I crave my reflection's sad eyes.

Critical of each flaw
that you mentioned.

Concentrated—
    "You're beautiful,"
    I speak out loud.

I watch my eyes light up
playful beauty, shining
and then I remember your words.

The light in my eyes gone
as quickly as it had come.

I crave my reflection's spark.

Critical of your effect.

Black and White

I dream in black and white
in good and bad
in wrong and right.
I dream in ideas
of pleasure and pain
of strenuous effort
and tenuous vain.
I can create the illusion
of our souls in my mind.
When I dream of you and I
we can't both be kind.
There's a contrasting fusion
one's dark and one's light.

And yet my dreams don't have color
they have *you and I.*

Busy

Days used to go by faster
when I was busy.
Now every day is faster
my mind is busy.

Busy asking
>   *How could he?*
Busy asking
>   *How could I let him?*
Busy asking
>   *What is my limit?*
Busy asking
>   *Did he already cross it?*

How Would They Know

Smiling over tears
so I won't let anyone near.
If I don't talk, they won't know.
Just keep progress flowing
suppress the torment,
  but it's growing

I'm sorry I said something
but I didn't say everything.
I don't know how to form
your darkness into words.
I just need to vent
but I'm afraid to be heard.

Another day fades to black
waiting for your next attack.
Can I call it that? It's not *that* bad.
They don't know.

I know you're like this, I don't believe it.
They wouldn't understand
they don't know what you mean to me.
I'll stay a little longer
      just in case you change.

Rainbow

Bruises show their colors;
purple, blue, red, and black.
Bruises show their true colors;
but they cannot speak
so no one listens.

Blue Eyes

Your sky-blue eyes
that whisked me away
in the clouds
are the same
tumultuous ocean-blue eyes
that made me drown.

His Name

My first tattoo, his name.
When did it come to represent
the names that he called me?

When did it come to represent pain?
Slammed into a wall and dragged
pulled hair, ringing ears.

When did it come to represent fear?
An accident, he will change
the clink of a gun.

When did it come to represent panic?
Running to the closest door that locks,
slumped down, choking on the air.

When did it come to represent dread?
This isn't who he really is,
he'll be mad at himself, he loves me.

When did it come to represent excuses?
Apologies, gifts, kisses,
he's just been stressed.

When did it become abuse?

Mundane

When I first met you
you lit a passionate flame
deep inside of me.
I said you were dangerous,
I meant that loving you so fiercely
would be dangerously hard
for us to maintain
this wild blaze.
You invoke in me the strongest emotions
and invoke in me my sweetest devotions.
And so, I prepared myself
for a comfortable mundane,
I would love you all the same.
But you were able to burn brightly,
dangerously stronger even, nightly.
I would love you all the same—
until I was engulfed in flames.

Nothing about you was mundane
it was the strongest love, loss,
and pain.

Panic Disorder

Silence filled
with the sound
of blood rushing
in my ears
the loud empty,
focused fear.
I could scream
no one would hear
I can't drop
a single tear
I can't scream,
focused fear.
No one can hear
it's just the blood rush
in my ears.

Numb Tide

I drink to drown
in the numb tide
as I sink down
my pain can hide.

Giving up
in vain,
I tried.

I try to drown
but I resurface
I know I have to
have a purpose.

But all I am
are cold,
wet bones
as I sink down
I feel alone.

Left to drown
in the numb
tide.

Blanket

You wore my trust
like a blanket
to comfort yourself
and took it off
when you were warm.

Cigarette Burns

Hot coffee
dripping into the pot
morning clarity
I wish it would stop.
Press my hand firmly
against scalding ceramic
full black coffee mug—
I clench tight as I panic
indulge the discomfort
of cigarette burns.
I trigger myself
until it doesn't hurt.
Pain, memories,
flashbacks are the worst
morning clarity
                    — *it still hurts.*

Bully

Bully, insult me;
with negative attention
I feel affection.

I am your safe place
to decompress your rage
I am an outlet.

Bury Me in Sand

Bury me in sand
deep in the ground
push me with your hand
until I can't hear a sound.
I'll be silent,
choking on sand.
You'll feel taller,
more of a man.
Leave me, I wanted it.
I'll dig my way out.
But as soon as I do,
sand pours from my mouth.
Bury me in sand,
I'll say it again.
And just like that,
I've dug my own hole
       again.

Step Ladder

Degrade me
        the lower that I feel
Betray me
        the higher you climb
Humiliate me
        upwards on your
Berate me
        narcissist
Isolate me
        step lad—
Silence me
        der

Disassociate

Sometimes reality
feels like a nightmare
and waking up
feels like I'm falling asleep.

Nothing hurts inside of dreams
so that's all my life is,
that's all it can be.

Just one elaborate,
       endless,
       bad dream.

A Safe Place

He doesn't greet me with "Hello," anymore.
He says, "You are crazy, take your pills!"
Antidepressants. I never needed them
before, I was never this sad before.
Reluctantly I swallow them whole. They
help me not feel the sorrow in my soul.

This crude presence of his makes my
nervous body tight. I hope he's in a good
mood, but what is good for him, right? I see
a smile on his face, he won't break anything
tonight. He'll ask me if I cleaned, I didn't do
it right. Even though I also worked, anything
to fight.

I think he might feel insecure. As he picks
away at me. He says, "You will never find
another man like me." I allow the way his
affliction feels. I've lost count of my
prescription pills.

The bad is always wrestling with the good.
I let this man do everything; hurt, scare,
demean. That's why letting him go should
have been necessary ease.

It was easier to stay comfortable, and not do
something new. Even though my
comfortable had become *undeniable abuse.*

I did not leave with ease or grace, I left with
guilt, shame, and grief. Leaving something
I'd known so long, did not feel like relief.
Daily I had asked myself, what my limit
would be.

The answer to my question wasn't what I
had thought; I assumed I'd either be dead,
hospitalized, or medically distraught.

I left in shock to be alive.
But it wasn't guaranteed.
Staying gone did not feel
like necessary ease.

I had left before.
I had left before, again.
Repeat until my sanity was as thin
                    as my bruised skin.

I refused to take any more.

"You are crazy, take your pills!"
Turns out, it wasn't me.

I haven't heard those words in months
I haven't felt the damage to my soul
I haven't felt like I'm stuck
      shell shocked in survival mode.
I'm in a different headspace
      no longer filling a devoid hole.
I just needed a safe place
         so I could feel whole.

BROKEN

Broken

Leaving is hard,
healing is hard.
But it's a wonderful thing
to be lost in the right direction.

Sometimes leaving will make you feel
guilty, overreactive, or dramatic.
Denying everything.
Sometimes leaving will make you feel like
what you had to go through was unfair.
Someone should have helped you.
Angry at everything.
Sometimes leaving will make you feel like
things will change if you do something
different because it's your one true love.
Bargaining everything.
Sometimes leaving will make you feel
indifferent, or tears will spill uncontrollably.
Depressed about everything.
Sometimes leaving will make you feel
relieved, excited, strong, and full of
potential to reclaim your life.
Acceptance for everything.

Sometimes leaving will make you grieve.

Silence

The silence is loud
after the storm that you left
there is quiet.
I don't remember
what this felt like.

I don't remember
who I am.

In this silence I am asking:
who am I?
Like thunder in my brain
I don't remember.

Tsunami

Thick depression
swirls around me
like a tsunami
draining
back into the sea.
It's everywhere
that I need to be
and everywhere
that I can see.
     Pulling me.

Leave Now

I just want my hands to stop shaking
when I hear your voice in my head
echoes of an entire life
where I was yours
your property
trapped
leave
now
trapped
inside my mind
haunting my entire life
I still hear your voice in my head
I just want my hands to stop shaking

Narcissist

I exhaled air
into a love,
that had the chance—
but would never breathe.

I miss a love that we never had
a fictional love that will never be.
I grieve this love as deeply as death
because I devoted a lifetime's worth
of tears, bruises, stress, hope, and
forgiveness.

I was chasing the love from our beginning
and when I caught up it was in pieces. I
would take what I was given and chase the
next piece.

Enough to keep me satisfied,
enough to keep me starving.

Now you're gone, and all of these intense
feelings, they should all be gone too. But
they linger in your absence. Now alone, I
must try healing.

So I can move on.

You never struggled with any of this.

I Miss Me

I miss me.
The me I was before you.

I fused my identity into *us*.
Without you,
who am I now?
If I'm not half of us
I'm just the broken half.

I miss me.
The me I was before you
made me feel
like I could never be whole.

Haunt

Your spirit can haunt me
it will not scare me
your voice in the walls
your memory radiating.

I see your eyes
when mine close
it will not scare me.

I'm used to it
your presence has haunted me
since before our last goodbye.

Grandeur

Delusions of grandeur,
misplaced aggressions,
words of slander;
echoes
in my
mind.

Pieces

Loving you
I lost pieces of myself
that I can't get back
and all I gained for myself
are panic attacks.

Alcohol

I read that drinking is bad for healing
from a particularly upsetting event,
it delays the mind's ability to process feeling
and just postpones one's ability to lament.
Death, love, a relationship lost,
promises void and null and irreparable—
thick heartache with an eternal cost
waiting to fully feel grief sounds preferable.
I'll not drink for a spell,
and run through emotional hell.
But sometimes an escape is what I need
because temporary relief is all it can be
now that I've lost someone so dear to me
a sober reality I never wanted to see.

Healing

Broken is comfortable
broken is
the closest thing left
to you

　　—and yet, I long for healing.

The Roaring Ocean

Always gasping for air,
like my lungs can't be satisfied.
A lightheaded affair
after barely surviving the tide.
The coastal flow pulls me in,
and away from you at last.
It cleanses me of your sin,
but it can't absolve our past.
Loving you I was drowning,
rocking in the waves—
holding my breath and counting,
washing up inside of caves
never free, always trapped.
The salty breeze is callous
my tender skin now chapped
surrounded by your malice.
And yet— I want for you to return to me.
Not the roaring ocean that you are,
but return to me as the calm sea.
I know serene waters are out too far,
and so, alone on the shore I will be,
aware that your current would drown me.

Past Self

If I could speak to my past self today
I wouldn't say you hurt me in arduous ways.
I wouldn't tell her that I would stay.

I would tell her how to leave.

She would think the first time was the last.
Oh for her, you would be over so fast.

I wouldn't tell her how cynical
                            a lover can be.
That's something I wish
                            didn't live with me.

I Still Haven't Slept

I would like a sliver of that sleep
that you seem to get so well
only the devil could sleep comfortably
knowing he made others burn in hell.

Best Wishes

I hope your actions
stare back at you
in the mirror
and you see yourself
as the monster
you showed me
and I wish nothing
but happiness for you
plagued in guilt
and an inability
to be satisfied
I hope you're constantly
unfulfilled and frightened.

Grow

I am buried deep in the dirt
my tears in the cold, moist soil.
Bruised, black, and hurt;
one ray of sunlight
I grow a vine
          I was a seed the entire time.

Identity

Losing my identity
in a sea of lost entities.
Smiling at a song you know,
laughing at my own joke.
Not knowing my favorite music
or my own sense of humor;
disassociated to survive.
I lived,
and now I'm lost inside.
Trying on habits,
like I used to try on shoes.
Ask me what I want,
but I'll always look to you.
Tell me what I like, I'll like it.

Trying

Sometimes I feel healed
other times I can't feel.

Guarded, protective numbness.
Depressive shutdown, glumness.

A hollow heart of stone.
Just want to be alone.

Can't look in the mirror,
blurred memories clearer.

Tomorrow I want back my identity,
today I'm disheveled by your entity.

Flames

I never played with matches,
I didn't want to get burned.
But you were the perfect match
and now I'm on fire.

Every Lifetime

I will find you
        in every lifetime
and I will leave you
        in every lifetime
each time
        more tragic than the last
                — *we're almost done.*

Forever

I used to cling to
the thought of forever
dreading your death
or mine
even then our souls
would stay twined.
Wedding vows
plans for our ashes
mixed together
in a rusty tin
as our time passes.
But it never did
and it never will.
You forgot to value me
for my worth;
broken doors and broken words
promises to change
break some more
promise in vain
but you won't break me anymore.

But damn, if I am not lost
in search of a new forever.

Regression

An endless summer rain
it falls in the same spot
the same place, the same time.
It pools into depressions,
it runs into oceans.
The ripples create a symphony
they create an entire life.
An endless summer rain
the ocean was polluted
the freeze took over
but not in that summer.
An endless summer rain
it falls in the same spot
the same place, the same time.

RESILIENCE

Resilience

Leaving feels like dying,
until it felt like being reborn.

This is the most important chapter and the
least painful one. Resilience feels like
safety, peace, and self-discovery.
You will live with your past,
but it will not live with you.

.

It's the time when you can walk alone,
relieved to be your biggest critic, but
choosing to love yourself instead.

Her Load

She could look at you
with starlight in her eyes
and nature in her smile.
She could speak the wind,
in any direction you wanted.
She did these things not for you,
but for her.
She carried the Earth on her shoulders,
the weight sifting it into her.
And so she wore her favorite parts,
dripping dew as she journeyed,
planting seeds of lust
to lighten her load.
But she kept the parts she hated,
as to not leave any on her path,
they became her burden
and she bared them,
heavy inside of her.

Worth

After years of getting hurt,
not knowing my worth,
expecting the worst;
I have to relearn
what I deserve.
And seek it
in return.

Heart of Gold

Maybe she was born with a heart of gold
or maybe,
it was torn from the trauma she holds.
Her heart was broken, ripped apart
she mended it herself,
alone in the dark.
That's what she's used to,
fixing mistakes
wondering how much more
she can take.
So when she sewed it together,
she decided to use
a golden thread
of virtue
— *trauma as a character builder.*

Battle

I wish I could thank you
for the love that we shared.

I can only thank you
for the love I was spared.

You wasted so much time
showing what love is not.

I can only thank you
for the battle we fought.

Stay

He told me
he would kill me.
He told me
to kill me.
He told me
every reason I should die.

I chose to stay.

Now I get to find out
        why.

Progress

To love a troubled man
was fearful at best;
at worst, I was stuck fixing
the mess that he left.
I became used to it;
the consistent distaste,
steady disappointment
nothing new to face.
He scared me then,
and he scares me now.
Freedom is constricting
stuck asking, how?
How to move on,
how to find out what's next?
How not to feel lonely
in a half-empty bed?
How do I live
not knowing what's next?

*The fear of new things is grim
but not as bad as my fear of him.*

Risen

I have risen
purpose from the ashes
of a fire I did not light.
More familiar as time passes
with the reckless burning fight
I know how to ignite
         a destructive force at my will.

I know how to ignite
with the hopeless yearning to fight
I choose to heal as time passes.
My fire will not light
purpose into the ashes;
I have risen.

Self Apology

I am sorry
that you thought you deserved it,
thought you were only worth it.

You were worth more.

I am sorry that you were too trusting,
and now you struggle with adjusting.

I am not sorry that you loved deeply,
I am sorry you protected yourself weakly,
but now you are stronger.

You are now the strongest
version of yourself
that you have ever been.
I hope that this is the strongest
you will ever need to be.

I am sorry that you were loved wrong,
I am not sorry that you are now strong.

Don't Let the Hard Days Win

Your score
for surviving
bad days
is still
perfect to none
                    —*you're winning.*

Hope

As soon as my hope fades
and I start to slip
I see a sign
and I gain my grip.
The universe provides
and my karma is strong
when I feel alone
I am guided along.
The universe is relentless,
forgiving, and inspired
twisted with irony
and hot with desire.

Dry Dirt

Tears fall from my eyes,
raindrops fall from my skies
saturated in a flourish of green.

Rain fills my Earth, the parts that I've seen.
It fills this dry dirt, loose particles,
I'm covered in a myriad of loose articles.
That I can't shake off, can't wash off.

The dry dirt that follows me,
unwelcomely clings to me.
The dry dirt is now stained.
Followed by abundance I never feigned,
a vibrantly green load of life.

A year with no drought, no strife,
it quenched my thirst, a welcomed sight
it filled wells without a fight.

A colossal abundance of rain
thriving after so much pain.
A refreshment
to quench my dehydrated thirst,
after you desiccated me the absolute worst,
in a painful profusion of your dry dirt.

That I shake off, I wash off.

Dear PTSD

Violet echoes in my ears
happy that my mind can't hear
blue depression, red rage
threaten to mix inside my brain.
My memories are a broken record
playing splinters
of destructive splendor.
I still hear you
when I close my eyes
but it does not affect me this time.

Jewel

Valuable to none
was your creeping inner thought
at least I'm valuable to one
is a lesson you were taught.

Suffer, like one of love's fools.
Then buffer out the scratches
because you are a jewel.

If there's only one collector
interested in you
be your own protector,
and make that person you.

Weakness

There is power
in weakness
when you've finally
succumbed
to your demons
you can air out
each struggle
internal and flesh
you can identify
each strength
and your ability
to deflect.
There is power
in weakness
if you survive
you will understand
your own ability
to fight for your life.

To Save Me

I left to save me
but I didn't realize that
until I felt safe.

Disappointment

Stop looking for light
in the darkest of places
the night oozes comfort
and you're being complacent.
Change is uncomfortable
for better or worse
the only promise that matters
is to put yourself first.

Wants and Needs

You once promised me an eternity
a flickering candle on the table,
a gray complexion for us both,
a fleeting moment; unstable.
You once promised me an eternity
for us to forever loathe
our wants burned for it
        — I know better now.

My Entirety

Make me feel seen
drape me with light.
Paint me as a kaleidoscope
in the brazen dim of the night.
Blue depression, yellow hope.
Passionate fuchsia
sets me apart,
blended to black
from pain in my heart.
I'm a colorful composite of art
beautifully blended in every part,
a multifaceted masterpiece.

Reminder

He broke your boundaries.

It is not your fault.
It was not your fault.
It will never be your fault.

You've rebuilt those boundaries
they're stronger now.

Love Yourself

I hope you choose
to love yourself
the way
you always hoped
he would.

Finally

I never wanted to heal
so I kept reliving it in my mind—
the ways I was hurt
and it was like the hot summer sun
burning in my chest.
Until one day the hurt was gone.
I was numb, like cold fingertips
while it hailed. My own comfort,
secondary to the thunderous storm
brought on by memories.
That day, every feeling was gone.
I never wanted to heal
and so I embraced the numb,
blending in like a wildflower
in the autumn rain.
Until one day it was back
the hurt was back—
as hot as the sun and as cold as the ice
all at once. But it wasn't in my fingers
and it wasn't in my chest.
Finally one day,
I was a hearty dandelion
decidedly growing in the rain.
I learned how to return
from the desolate storm.